THE CONQUEST OF
EVEREST

Mike Rosen

Illustrated by Doug Post

The Bookwright Press
New York · 1990

Great Journeys

First published in the
United States in 1990 by
The Bookwright Press
387 Park Avenue South
New York, NY 10016

First published in 1989 by
Wayland (Publishers) Limited
61 Western Road, Hove
East Sussex BN3 1JD, England

Library of Congress Cataloging-in-Publication Data
Rosen, Mike.
   The conquest of Everest/by Mike Rosen.
      p.   cm. — (Great journeys)
   Summary: Surveys the various attempts to climb Mount Everest and
gives a detailed account of the successful climb made by Hillary and
Tenzing.
   Bibliography: p.
   Includes index.
   ISBN 0–531–18319–X
   1. Mountaineering—Everest, Mount (China and Nepal)—History–
—Juvenile literature.   [1. Mountaineering.   2. Everest, Mount
(China and Nepal)]   I. Title.   II. Series.
GV199.44.E85R67   1990
796.5'22'095496—dc20   89–9688
                                                                    CIP
                                                                     AC

Typeset by DP Press Ltd, Sevenoaks, Kent
Printed in Italy by G. Canale & C.S.p.A.

Frontispiece *On May
29, 1953, Tenzing
Norgay (pictured here)
and Edmund Hillary
became the first climbers
to reach Everest's
summit.*

Cover *The summit of
Everest was not
conquered until 1953.
This magnificent
mountain continues to be
thought of as the ultimate
challenge by climbers
from all over the world.*

Contents

The Challenge of Everest

One June afternoon in 1921 George Mallory and Guy Bullock stood on a hilltop in the Himalayas. Ahead of them, partly hidden by swirling clouds, lay the highest mountain in the world – Everest. As the clouds parted, Mallory got his first view of the slopes and summit of this mighty mountain. His ambition was to reach its summit.

In fact the summit of Everest stood unclimbed for another thirty-two years. By that time twenty people, including George Mallory, had died trying to climb the mountain, which is one of the most dangerous in the world. Fierce storms, biting cold and huge avalanches are just a few of the obstacles that face those who accept its challenge.

Everest is shaped like a pyramid, with three long ridges separating its sheer faces. The summit stands at 8,848 m (29,000 ft) above sea level, surrounded by a range of other mountains almost as high. It was first mapped by the British Survey of India in the 1850s when, unable to find out its local name, surveyors named the mountain after their leader, Sir George Everest.

At altitudes above 8,000 m (26,000 ft) there is very little oxygen in the air. Starved of oxygen, blood thickens, threatening to block the veins and cause paralysis or death.

Without a proper blood supply, brain cells die faster than the body can replace them. Climbers can suffer memory loss, make wrong decisions, and lose control of their reactions.

Above Everest, seen from the southwest. This side of Everest was first visited by foreign climbers in 1950.

Their muscles cannot recover from exercise because strength is lost quickly. After several days at high altitude even a short walk takes great energy.

Another danger is dehydration. Thin dry air removes the moisture from a climber's body. Without water, the body weakens rapidly. On the cold, windswept snow slopes of Everest, climbers often forget their need for large amounts of water. Many have come close to death as a result.

On high mountains at night, or when a storm is raging, the temperature can drop far below freezing. Even with warm clothes, climbers can suffer from frostbite. This condition freezes the flesh and stops the blood from circulating; toes and fingers are most at risk. Even without frostbite, the cold is dangerous to a climber. It numbs the fingers and dulls reactions, making accidents more likely.

Glaciers must be crossed to reach the slopes and ridges of Everest. Deep crevasses split the glaciers, some of which are hidden beneath a thin covering of snow. On the mountain itself avalanches are a constant risk. At the tops of ridges the snow may form a cornice over a drop of as much as a thousand meters (3,300 ft) to the glaciers below. A cornice may collapse under the weight of a climber. Of every ten climbers who go to such high altitudes one will die.

Below *George Mallory (seated, far left) and Guy Bullock (standing, third from left) with the other 1921 Everest expedition members at their base camp.*

People of Everest

Left The north side of Everest seen from the ruins of the Rongbuk monastery in Tibet. In the 1920s the monastery was still in use.

It was not until many years after Mount Everest had been mapped that its local name was discovered. The people who lived on the lower slopes of Everest called it Chomolungma, which means Goddess Mother of the Earth.

Everest lies on the border of two countries – Nepal and Tibet. Tibet has been governed by China since 1949, but for many years before the Chinese took control, Tibet was ruled by Buddhist monks. The first British expeditions to Everest traveled through Tibet. They found it to be a land of great contrasts. While the religious rulers were very wealthy, the people of Tibet lived in terrible poverty, scratching a bare living from farming.

The Buddhist people of Tibet believed that living in the mountains could bring them closer to religious truth. They built monasteries at the base of the glaciers running down from Everest in the Rongbuk valley. Today the great monastery of

Above While many Tibetans lived in extreme poverty, their leader, the Dalai Lama, lived in this magnificent palace (the Potala) in Lhasa. The Potala is still the center of Tibetan Buddhism.

Rongbuk lies in ruins. Under Chinese rule the Tibetan people were encouraged to overthrow the power of monasteries. Their religious leader, the Dalai Lama, fled and many of the monasteries were destroyed.

On the southern side of Everest lies Nepal. Although Nepal's religion is officially Hindu, the people who live around Everest are largely Buddhist. The two main groups of people living near Everest are the Bhotias and the Sherpas. Both are used to living at high altitude – they normally live between 3,000 and 4,000 m (10,000 and 13,000 ft) above sea level. For centuries they have lived as farmers and traders. The southern foothills are warmer and more fertile than the northern slopes, and the Nepalese live in greater comfort than their Tibetan neighbors.

Sherpas have proved to be excellent climbers on Everest; a Sherpa, Tenzing Norgay, was one of the two men who made the first successful ascent to the summit. Many Everest expeditions have depended on the work of Sherpas. The early expeditions did not pay them well or look after their safety, but today, the Nepalese government insists that Sherpas be given better pay, safety equipment and insurance against injury or death.

Like the Tibetans, the Sherpas believe that Everest is a sacred place. Before they set foot on the mountain, or stay in a camp on its slopes, religious rituals must be performed.

Every expedition is blessed in a ceremony performed by local monks. Campsites must be protected by a sprinkling of holy water and flowers.

Sherpa life is changing. Everest and the Himalayas are popular among tourists, and, with the money earned, Sherpas have built hotels and restaurants. Farming has become much less popular, and more and more Sherpas earn a living from the tourist industry.

Above A Nepalese monk in the valleys below Everest. He has made his fire with yak dung, the usual fuel in these high mountains.

The First Expeditions

In 1921, British climbers led the first expedition to Everest. It passed through India and Tibet to the mountain's north side. Over several weeks of exploration, the climbers observed Everest from many viewpoints. Finally, they found a possible route up the mountain. From the main Rongbuk valley they could enter the East Rongbuk glacier. This glacier led to the North Col, a dip in the North Ridge. The North Ridge would take them to the Northeast Ridge and from there it looked like an easy climb to the summit.

One thing was clear; no attempt to climb this route could succeed without careful planning. A system of camps and supply dumps had to be set up at various points to provide support and shelter for those on the mountain. At each camp the climbers would need enough food, oxygen and cooking equipment to survive. If too much were carried up, precious time and effort would be wasted, but without enough supplies failure would be certain.

The next year, 1922, another British expedition followed the route leading to the North Col and set up camp. From there a party of four climbers (George Mallory, Major Edward Norton, Major Henry T. Morshead and Howard Somervell) set out to climb the North Ridge. After camping overnight on the slopes of the spur, Morshead was too

Left The team members of the 1922 expedition before leaving for Everest. Standing from second on the left are Norton, Mallory, Somervell and Morshead. George Finch is seated, far right.

weak to continue the climb. Mallory and the others struggled on. Eventually, just below the Northeast Ridge, they too decided to turn back.

Back at their tents they found Morshead seriously ill due to frostbite and dehydration. It was plain they had to get down to the North Col camp that night. Carefully, the climbers began their descent. Fresh snow hid the route and made the rocks slippery. Wisely, they linked themselves together with rope for safety. When one climber fell, pulling two others off their feet, Mallory thrust his ice ax deep into the snow, and held the rope firm. His quick action saved his companions. When they reached the North Col camp they were safe, but exhausted.

Another group of three climbers, led by George Finch, made a second attempt on the summit. This time the expedition used oxygen equipment. Finch believed that breathing extra oxygen would help lessen the strain on their bodies during the climb. Despite being trapped in their tents by a storm for two nights, Finch's party climbed almost 200 m (650 ft) higher than Mallory's group had previously managed.

These first mountaineers learned much about the difficulties and dangers of climbing Everest. They had felt the effects of working at high altitude for long periods, and knew the dangers of frostbite and dehydration. Tents, clothing and cooking equipment had been severely tested. A

Above and left George Finch demonstrating the oxygen equipment during the march through Tibet, 1922, and an expedition member wearing breathing equipment.

possible route to the summit had been explored to a height of 8,200 m (27,000 ft). Also, Finch's party had shown the benefits of breathing extra oxygen while climbing at high altitude.

Above Climbing the North Col, 1922. The climbers are roped together so that if one slips the others can stop him from falling too far.

Mallory and Irvine

A British team returned to Everest in 1924. Once again, the expedition passed through Tibet to the Rongbuk valley. Base Camp was established near the Rongbuk monastery, and Camp Two was set up on the East Rongbuk glacier. Snowstorms and extreme cold slowed down work on the higher camps, but finally, at the end of May 1924, Camp Six was built high on the North Ridge.

On June 4, 1924, Major Norton and Howard Somervell left Camp 6, heading for the summit. It was a fine day, with little wind. Despite this, the biting cold left the climbers shivering each time they stopped for a rest. By noon Norton and Somervell had reached the Great Couloir, a steep gully. This passage would take them to the base of the final summit pyramid, but Somervell could climb no farther. His throat was frostbitten, and he could hardly breathe. Norton continued alone for another hour. Finally the strain of climbing alone and unroped on dangerous slabs of rock forced him to turn back.

Two days later, George Mallory and Andrew Irvine strapped on their oxygen equipment and left Camp 4. In 1922, Mallory had opposed the use of oxygen, but now he was convinced it would help them reach the summit. With the boost of extra oxygen, Mallory and Irvine climbed easily to Camp 5 and Camp 6. On June 8, 1924, they set off for the summit. Around midday another climber, Noel Odell, saw Mallory and Irvine on the Northeast Ridge, crossing a

Below Camp 2 on the East Rongbuk Glacier, pictured in 1924.

Left The remains of an avalanche on a snow slope. Avalanches were a constant danger on the slopes of the North Col.

patch of snow beneath some rocks. They vanished from his view, then reappeared a few minutes later on top of the ridge, above the Second Step. Odell watched until clouds covered the scene and then made his way back to the safety of Camp 4.

Late into the night the members of the expedition waited for Mallory and Irvine, watching anxiously for any movement on the moonlit slopes of Everest. The next day Odell climbed above Camp 6, searching for any sign of his friends. He found nothing, and bad weather forced him to abandon the search. The climbers knew that Mallory and Irvine would never return.

No one knows whether Mallory and Irvine reached the summit. They were climbing strongly when Odell saw them, but the last part of the Northeast Ridge is difficult and dangerous. In 1933 Irvine's ice ax was found on the Northeast Ridge, and in 1980 the body of an unknown man, dressed in 1920s clothing, was found below the ridge on the Northeast Terrace. If this body was Irvine, he must have slipped coming down the mountain. No trace of Mallory has ever been found. The mystery remains – were Mallory and Irvine the first men to reach Everest's summit?

Above George Mallory *(left) and Andrew Irvine (right) disappeared on Everest in 1924. It is not known whether they managed to reach the summit. In 1933 Irvine's ice ax was found on the Northeast Ridge.*

A New Approach

After the deaths of Mallory and Irvine, the rulers of Tibet refused to allow climbers onto Everest until 1933. Between 1933 and 1939, four major expeditions used the well-known route past the North Col, and although the summit remained unclimbed, the expeditions learned much about climbing and working at high altitudes.

Everest expeditions stopped in 1939 when World War II began. After the war, Tibet was invaded by the Chinese, and its frontiers were closed to Europeans. The traditional route to Everest was blocked. Then, in 1951, the government of Nepal allowed a British expedition to approach Everest from the south side.

The expedition of 1951 was led by the famous explorer Eric Shipton. He had been on all the British Everest expeditions of the 1930s, and had explored the western slopes of the mountain in 1938. His aim in 1951 was to explore the southern slopes of Everest and find a possible route to the summit. The journey to Everest through Nepal led through forest valleys and fertile meadows full of alpine

Above *Eric Shipton.*

Below *Sherpas using ladders to cross a crevasse in the Khumbu Icefall.*

flowers. Shipton and his party reached Everest with their energies at full strength.

During October 1951, Shipton's climbers moved up the Khumbu glacier. Although they were unable to reach the slopes of Everest, they got close enough to see a possible route to the summit. If climbers could get through the Khumbu Icefall into the Western Cwm they could cross the lower face of Lhotse mountain and reach the South Col of Everest. From there, they could follow the South Ridge to the summit.

The first climbers to try the new south route were a Swiss party that attempted the ascent in 1952. Led by Raymond Lambert, the Swiss climbers were well organized. They found a path through the Khumbu Icefall, crossed the Lhotse Face and reached the South Col without difficulty. From there, Raymond Lambert set out for the summit with the Sherpa, Tenzing Norgay.

At first the climb went well, but above 8,500 m (28,000 ft) the effects of altitude began to weaken them. Already they had climbed higher on Everest than any earlier climber. As their strength disappeared, each step became an effort. Finally, at 8,600 m (28,000 ft), they could go no farther. Exhausted, they staggered back to their tents on the South Col.

Another attempt was made to reach the summit. This time, the Swiss climbers came within 250 m (820 ft) of their goal before defeat. Afterward,

Lambert felt they should have built another camp between the Western Cwm and the South Col. The 900-m (2,950-ft) climb between these two points left the climbers too little strength for the push to the summit.

Below *This map shows the geographical location of Everest and the Himalayas.*

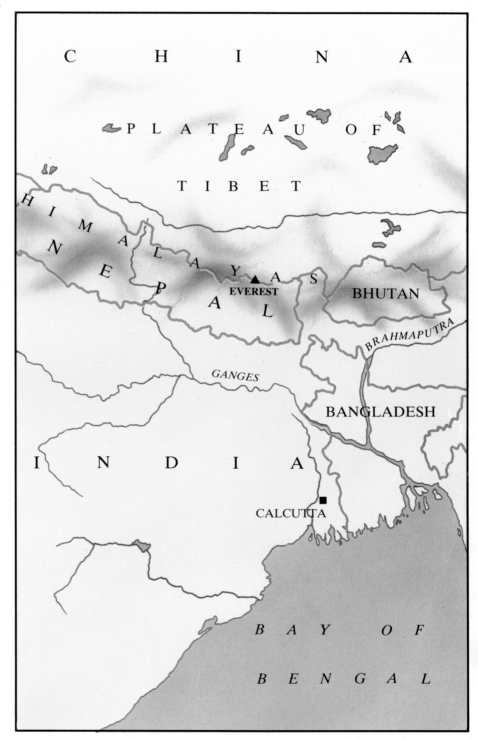

1953: Preparing for Everest

News of the Swiss climbers' attempts caused great excitement in Britain. It was clear that the route up Everest from the south promised good chances for success. The British expedition of 1953 could be the first to reach the summit. Preparations were begun.

Colonel John Hunt was chosen as expedition leader. Although Hunt had never been on Everest, he was an experienced climber. Even more important, he was excellent at organizing people. Using the lessons learned by previous expeditions, Hunt made precise plans about what supplies would be needed at each camp and how long it would take to carry them up there.

One lesson learned from the earlier Everest expeditions was

Above Tenzing Norgay (left) and Colonel John Hunt (right). Hunt led the 1953 expedition to Everest. Tenzing, who first climbed on Everest in 1938, had nearly reached the summit in 1952 with the Swiss climber Raymond Lambert.

Left Improved clothing and oxygen equipment gave the 1953 climbers more chance of success on Everest than the climbers of the 1920s and 1930s.

that climbing at high altitudes was made harder by the lack of oxygen in the thin air. Most climbers in the 1920s and 1930s had tried to climb Everest without the help of extra oxygen. The oxygen equipment of that time was heavy and often broke down. Some of the climbers on those expeditions also felt that to use oxygen equipment was cheating – if Everest could not be climbed without extra oxygen, then it should not be climbed at all.

By 1953, climbers were sure that Everest could not be climbed without the help of extra oxygen. There are only a few months each year when the weather is fine on Everest, and in that short time, climbers' bodies have little chance to get used to life at high altitude. An expedition must move fast and the use of extra oxygen makes the climbers' progress quicker.

During World War II oxygen equipment had improved. It was much lighter than the equipment used on Everest in the 1920s and 1930s, and far more reliable. Tests on pilots flying at high altitudes had shown its benefits. The 1953 expedition was determined to use all the help available.

Other equipment had also improved since the 1930s. Nylon, a new material in those days, meant that ropes and tents could be lighter and stronger. Clothing was specially designed for climbing at high altitude in freezing temperatures. The first climbers on Everest had worn ordinary clothes and climbing boots. By 1953, specialized down-filled jackets and pants made of waterproof fabrics had been developed. Newly designed climbing boots had air chambers in the soles to keep feet warm and dry.

1953: To the South Col

John Hunt and his team set off from Katmandu in March 1953. With them went over 8 tons of supplies and equipment, carried by 350 porters. The climbers marched through forests, valleys, and narrow gorges to the bottom of Everest, where Base Camp was set up on the Khumbu Glacier. Most of the porters were then sent home to their villages. Only the climbers, their Sherpa guides, and the mountain porters remained.

The first task was to cross the Khumbu Icefall. This is a jumble of crevasses and massive blocks of ice. These are part of the glacier, which is always moving. In the upper part of the Icefall, Hunt's climbers worked among towers of ice that could collapse at any time, crushing anyone caught beneath them. They had to wear crampons on their boots and cut steps with their ice axes to avoid slipping. As the climbers chipped at the ice towers, the ice fell into the deep crevasses far below.

Despite the dangers, a route was completed by the end of April. The supplies and equipment were carried through the Icefall into the Western Cwm. Advance Base Camp was built in the Western Cwm at the bottom of the Lhotse Face.

Right *The routes taken by three of the most significant Everest expeditions.*

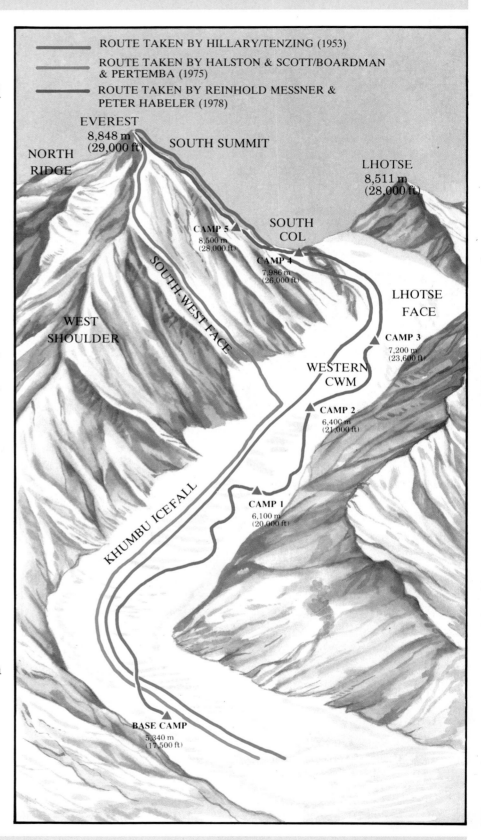

ROUTE TAKEN BY HILLARY/TENZING (1953)

ROUTE TAKEN BY HALSTON & SCOTT/BOARDMAN & PERTEMBA (1975)

ROUTE TAKEN BY REINHOLD MESSNER & PETER HABELER (1978)

EVEREST
8,848 m
(29,000 ft)

SOUTH SUMMIT

NORTH RIDGE

LHOTSE
8,511 m
(28,000 ft)

CAMP 5
8,500 m
(28,000 ft)

SOUTH COL

CAMP 4
7,986 m
(26,000 ft)

LHOTSE FACE

WEST SHOULDER

SOUTH-WEST FACE

CAMP 3
7,200 m
(23,600 ft)

WESTERN CWM

CAMP 2
6,400 m
(21,000 ft)

KHUMBU ICEFALL

CAMP 1
6,100 m
(20,000 ft)

BASE CAMP
5,340 m
(17,500 ft)

Above *The summit seen from the Lhotse Face. The Southeast Ridge runs down the center.*

The Lhotse Face is mostly hard ice. With crampons, ice axes and pitons to anchor their climbing-ropes, the climbers thought they would make good progress. However, the weather turned bad and heavy snow fell on the Lhotse Face. It hid the route as fast as the climbers built it, filling newly cut steps with fresh snow, and burying the safety-ropes. Fierce winds lashed across the bare slopes, the force of which almost blew the climbers off the mountain. Clinging desperately to the slippery ice, the climbers had little strength left for chipping steps or hammering pitons into the ice face.

On May 23, 1953, Colonel Hunt, Charles Evans, Tom Bourdillon and Da Namgyal spent a bitter night in Camp 7, halfway up the Lhotse Face. Howling winds battered the tents, and they could only sleep by breathing extra oxygen. The next day they struggled on in wind and snow.

At the South Col, weary from their climb, Hunt and his companions fought to put up their tents. On the stony ground, sheeted with ice, it was hard to stand upright. Finally, after an hour of struggle, two tents were safely put up. The climbers collapsed inside them, listening to the gale outside.

Above *Climbers moving up the Western Cwm toward the Lhotse Face.*

1953: So Near, So Far

Early in the morning of May 27 Charles Evans and Tom Bourdillon left the South Col camp. They climbed quickly for nearly two hours. Then their oxygen equipment began to fail – the valves were becoming frozen. Despite this, Evans and Bourdillon continued to climb. Around midday, they reached the South Summit. Less than 450 m (1,500 ft) away and only 90 m (300 ft) above them stood the peak of Mount Everest.

Just as success seemed to be theirs, Evans discovered a new problem with his oxygen supply. With the weather growing worse, the two climbers felt it would be dangerous to go on. They could not risk being caught in bad weather with no oxygen supply as darkness fell. Sadly they turned around and hurried back to the camp.

Back at the South Col, Evans and Bourdillon talked about the climb with Edmund Hillary and Tenzing Norgay, who had been chosen to make the second attempt. Tenzing Norgay had first climbed on Everest in 1935 with Shipton and had come close to the summit with Lambert in 1952. Edmund Hillary was a climber from New Zealand who had been on Everest with Shipton in 1951.

Evans and Bourdillon thought that it would take two days to reach the summit from the South Col. Tenzing Norgay knew a good place to pitch a tent just below the South Summit. On May 28 Tenzing and Hillary

Below As Hillary moved forward, Tenzing held him firm by burying his ice ax in the snow. If Hillary slipped, Tenzing would be able to keep him from falling far.

climbed from the South Col to this site. Early the next morning they stood on the South Summit.

They looked at the ridge ahead. To the right was the Kangshung Face, a sheer cliff dropping 3,000 m (1,000 ft) to the Kangshung Glacier. That side of the ridge was made up of huge cornices of snow. If Hillary and Tenzing moved onto one of these cornices, they would be in great danger; their weight could cause the unsupported snow to break free of the ridge, hurling them down Kangshung Face.

To avoid the cornices, Hillary and Tenzing had to keep to the left of the ridge. That meant crossing a long smooth slope of snow. If the snow were loose, or in unstable layers, an avalanche could drag them down the slope and over steep cliffs into the Western Cwm.

Nervously, Hillary tested the snow. It felt firm. Tenzing thrust his ice ax deep into the snow, and tied the climbing rope to it. Hillary tied himself to the other end of the rope and began to cut steps across the slope. After 10 m (30 ft) he stopped. Now it was Hillary's turn to dig his ice ax into the snow and hold the safety rope. Tenzing moved across the slope to join him. They moved on, each taking turns to anchor the rope firmly into the snow for safety.

Above *Hillary checks Tenzing's oxygen equipment. Although the air temperature on Everest is very cold, when the sun shines from a clear sky climbers can get too hot in their down jackets.*

1953: To the Summit

After an hour they had crossed the snow slope. A new obstacle lay before them; a rock step nearly 12 m (40 ft) high. They examined it closely. Its surface had been worn smooth by wind and snow, and no easy holds were visible. At low altitude, with pitons and plenty of time, they could have made a route up this step. At nearly 8,700 m (29,000 ft) they barely had the strength to move, and their oxygen supply would last only a few more hours. It looked as though Everest had won again.

Then Hillary saw a gap at the side of the step – a crack between the rock and a cornice of snow. Squeezing himself into the crack, Hillary called on his last store of strength. Kicking his crampons into the snow of the cornice and using every handhold he could find in the rock, he climbed slowly upward. Tenzing watched anxiously, afraid that the cornice would break away from the rock. Luckily, it held firm. Hillary dragged himself over the final ledge onto the top of the step and lay there for several minutes, gasping for breath. Even with the help of his oxygen supply, the effort of climbing the step had been tremendous. As soon as he recovered, Hillary held the rope while Tenzing scrambled up. This passageway is now called Hillary's Chimney.

The two climbers struggled on. Again and again they had to cut steps across slopes of snow or scramble over loose rocks. The ridge seemed to last forever. Each time they reached the top of a hump, they saw another beyond it. Excitement turned to

Below Hillary and
Tenzing on the summit.
After thirty-two years of
trying, climbers had
conquered Everest at last.

exhaustion, and each step was painful. Their muscles ached and their hearts and lungs strained to keep their bodies working. The climb became a test of their determination, but they refused to give in.

Suddenly Hillary saw that the ridge in front of him no longer led upward. He was looking down the north side of Everest.

Below him lay the North Col, the Rongbuk Glacier, and the ridge where Mallory and Irvine had last been seen in 1924. A little to his right was the summit of Everest. Two more steps and Hillary and Tenzing were standing on the top of the world's highest mountain.

They shook hands and hugged each other in relief and excitement. Both men looked around at the Himalayas stretched out beneath them. They photographed the view, then each other standing on the summit. Tenzing dug a small hole in the snow in which he placed some food as a gift to the spirits of the mountain, following his Buddhist beliefs. Hillary buried a crucifix as Colonel Hunt had requested. Then the two climbers left the summit.

Late that afternoon they walked into the South Col camp. The news flashed around the world. Thirty-two years after the first expedition Everest had at last been conquered.

Faces of Everest

After 1953, many mountaineers climbed the mountain by the South Col route. Four Swiss climbers reached the summit in 1956, followed in 1963 by three Americans and a Sherpa. Two years later, in 1965, an Indian expedition got as many as nine climbers to the top of Everest.

In 1954 a team including an American, Woodrow Sayre Wilson (a relative of former President Woodrow Wilson's), crossed from Nepal to Tibet in order to climb Everest from the north side. The climbers had not asked the permission of the Nepalese government, and, as a result of this, Nepal would not allow any climbers to cross their country in order to reach Everest for a period of two years.

In 1960 Chinese climbers followed the North Col route taken by the British expeditions of the 1920s. With the help of extra oxygen they reached the summit. Three years later, two Americans climbed to the top of Everest along the West Ridge. After this, climbers began to think about scaling the faces of Everest directly.

The Southwest Face was the first choice. In 1969 and 1970 Japanese climbers reached a height of 8,050 m (26,000 ft), despite being hit by small avalanches of stones. Another attempt on this face was made in 1972 by a small team led by the British climber Chris Bonington; they reached the same point as the Japanese team had done several years earlier.

Above On their way back from the summit, Scott and Haston had to spend the night in a snow cave. As the temperature fell far below freezing point they struggled to keep warm.

Bonington returned to the Southwest Face in 1975. With him were many of the climbers from the 1972 expedition. Special tents were used for the higher camps; these had a frame of metal poles that could be assembled easily in even the worst storm. The tent was strong enough to survive small avalanches of stones.

Bonington's climbers were soon ready to try for the summit. On September 24, 1975, Dougal Haston and Doug Scott set off. The climbers had already placed fixed safety ropes along the dangerous gullies of loose rock, and they moved across this section easily. Despite a fault in Haston's oxygen system, the two men reached Everest's summit at sunset. Unable to get back to their camp in the dark, Scott and Haston dug a snow cave. As the temperature fell to 30 degrees below freezing point, they fought to stay awake, rubbing their feet to prevent frostbite. Amazingly, they survived and got down safely the next day.

Then tragedy struck. Two more pairs of climbers tried to reach the summit. The first pair, Pete Boardman and Sherpa Pertemba, were successful, but on their way down from the summit they met Mick Burke climbing alone. Burke's partner, Martin Boysen, had given up the climb when his oxygen set broke down. Burke asked Boardman to go with him to the summit. Boardman was too tired, so Burke went on alone, while Boardman and Pertemba waited at the South Summit. While they waited, a storm blew up; Burke was never seen again.

During the 1980s Everest's other faces were also climbed. In 1983, six Americans reached the summit from the Kangshung Face, which is probably the hardest climb on Everest. In 1988, a British expedition also reached the summit by using this difficult route.

Women on Everest

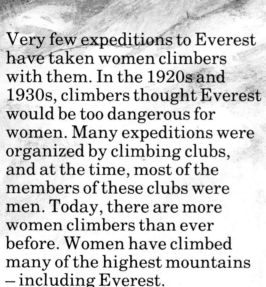

Very few expeditions to Everest have taken women climbers with them. In the 1920s and 1930s, climbers thought Everest would be too dangerous for women. Many expeditions were organized by climbing clubs, and at the time, most of the members of these clubs were men. Today, there are more women climbers than ever before. Women have climbed many of the highest mountains – including Everest.

In 1970 a Japanese woman, Setsuko Watanabe, climbed as far as the South Col. Five years later, in 1975, two expeditions raced to get the first woman climber to Everest's summit. One was a Chinese expedition, which included thirty-two women. This followed the old route past the North Col and up the Northeast Ridge. The other team in the race was a Japanese all-women team, which used the Hillary and Tenzing route through the South Col.

Both expeditions set up their Base Camp in the middle of March. By the beginning of May, the Japanese had built a camp on the Lhotse Face. On May 4 a huge avalanche sent massive blocks of ice crashing onto the tiny tents, and one climber, Junko Tabei, was trapped beneath an ice block. Its weight crushed her chest until she could hardly breathe. Somehow she managed to pull a knife from her pocket, cut a hole

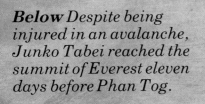

in the tentcloth, and call for help. Two Sherpas pushed the ice block away and dragged Junko from the tent.

On the north side of the mountain, the Chinese expedition made steady progress. By May 15, 1975, the climbers had only reached an altitude of 7,600 m (25,000 ft), because it is harder to climb Everest from the North Col route. That same day the Japanese built their last camp at 8,500 m (28,000 ft). Despite her injuries, Junko Tabei had been chosen to try for the summit. With her was the Sherpa guide Ang Tshering.

Tabei and Tshering left their tent at 5 am on May 16. Tabei was feeling the effects of her avalanche injuries. She felt exhausted and had to rest often. The rock and snow passageway of Hillary's Chimney nearly stopped her as she was not tall enough to reach all of the handholds. On the summit ridge the wind blew hard. Tabei crawled on knees and elbows over the rocks and snow. At last she reached the summit – the first woman to get there.

Eleven days later, nine Chinese climbers got to the top of Everest. Among them was a Tibetan woman called Phan Tog. Although Junko Tabei had reached the summit first, Phan Tog was the first woman to climb Everest from the north side. She had managed this despite gale-force winds and snowstorms, up slopes that had beaten many other climbers.

Alone on Everest

A lone climber on Everest faces great danger. There is no partner to hold the safety rope over difficult rocks or slippery ice, and one mistake could send a lone climber crashing down the slopes. The extra danger adds mental strain; without the support of other climbers it is easy to give up.

One person cannot build a series of camps and a route before trying to reach the summit. The tent and all the supplies needed have to be carried right to the summit and back. For this reason, a lone climber cannot use oxygen equipment – making the climb even tougher.

The first man to climb alone on Everest was Maurice Wilson. Wilson was a brave man but he had strange ideas. He planned to fly to Everest and crash-land as high on the mountain as possible. From there, he thought it would be an easy walk to the summit. Many people tried to warn him of the dangers but he ignored them. When he arrived in India, his plane was taken by the government so Wilson hiked to the slopes of Everest.

He managed to get as far as the North Col and tried to climb higher, but bad weather forced him back. All this time Wilson was starving himself, as he believed that by not eating he could purify his body. Once his body was pure, he thought, a holy energy would fill him and

Above *A solo climber does not have the support of the porters that are used by large expeditions.*

Below *Reinhold Messner achieved two Everest records. In 1978, with Peter Habeler, he reached the summit by the South Col route without using extra oxygen. In 1980 he climbed Everest's North Face alone – again without the help of oxygen equipment. This picture shows Messner during his expedition up K2 in 1979. He has climbed the fourteen highest peaks in the world – all over 8,000 m (26,000 ft) high – without using oxygen.*

carry him to Everest's summit. Sadly for Wilson this did not happen. Instead he got weaker every day and eventually he died of starvation in his tent.

In August 1980 climbers all over the world heard that the German climber Reinhold Messner had climbed Everest alone. To make his climb even more amazing, Messner had used the north route which had beaten so many great climbers before him. Earlier, in 1978, Messner had been the first to climb Everest without the help of extra oxygen. Now he had achieved that which climbers had thought impossible.

It took Messner just three days to reach Everest's summit from his Base Camp on the Rongbuk Glacier. He could not climb the North Ridge because of new snow and, to avoid it, he moved out onto the North Face of Everest. At night he dug a snow cave for shelter. On August 20, 1980, Messner stood on Everest's summit.

Messner's solo climb has never been repeated. Although they admire Messner's skill and bravery, most climbers prefer to climb Everest as part of a team. However, Messner's success started a new style of climbing Everest in smaller teams.

The Unclimbed Ridge

Today Everest presents one last challenge to climbers – the full length of the Northeast Ridge. Along this ridge stand some of the hardest obstacles on Everest, the fearsome Pinnacles. These are huge towers of rock coated in ice and snow. The only way past is to go over the top, for on each side there are sheer ice slopes.

In 1982 Chris Bonington led a small expedition to climb this ridge without extra oxygen. Despite careful acclimatization, the strains of working hard at high altitude affected them badly. Bonington was unable to climb above 8,000 m (26,000 ft), and another climber became very ill.

Only two climbers, Pete Boardman and Joe Tasker, were fit enough to go on. From their snow cave high on the ridge, they climbed to the base of the Pinnacles. That evening they talked to Chris Bonington on their radio sets, and the next day, Bonington watched Boardman and Tasker through a powerful telescope. He saw them climb the First Pinnacle, then move across a small col to the Second Pinnacle. The two men were climbing slowly on difficult rock, weary due to the effects of oxygen shortage.

The next day Boardman and Tasker were not seen on the ridge. Anxiously, Bonington scanned the rocks with his telescope and sent messages on his radio. There was no reply to his worried calls, and nothing moved on the Pinnacles. For two more days they searched for the missing climbers. Sadly they realized that Boardman and Tasker had joined the long list of those killed on Everest.

Another expedition to the Northeast Ridge in 1985 was beaten by bad weather. The ridge still remains unclimbed. Elsewhere on Everest, several expeditions each year try to reach the summit but often they fail. Everest is still a very difficult mountain to climb, with or without the help of oxygen, and by 1986, 103 climbers had died on its slopes.

Sad to say, so many people now climb on Everest that its wild beauty is in danger. Climbers have left rubbish at all their campsites; empty gas cylinders, cans of food, and tattered tents lie in the snow. The first Everest expedition members used melted snow to make drinks. Any climber doing that today on Everest's lower slopes is likely to get a serious stomach illness from melting dirty snow. Many climbers believe that Everest should be open to fewer expeditions.

Despite these problems, the challenge of the world's highest mountain continues to attract climbers. For those who reach the top, like the 1988 Australian expedition, it is unforgettable.

Above *Two members of the 1971 International Everest Expedition – one of many expeditions that have failed to reach the summit of Everest.*

Left *The North Face of Everest. The Pinnacles of the Northeast Ridge are on the far left.*

29

Glossary

Acclimatization The process of getting used to new conditions.

Altitude The height above sea level.

Avalanche A mass of snow or rocks that has broken away from the mountain face and rolls down its slopes.

Col A strip of land or a ridge connecting two formations, such as mountain peaks.

Cornice A mass of snow overhanging a cliff edge.

Crampons Metal spikes on a frame that fits on a climbing boot.

Crevasse A split in the surface of a glacier. Often crevasses are very deep.

Cwm, also called a cirque A steep-sided semi-circular depression, formed by glacial ice, which is found in mountainous regions and often contains a lake. Cwm is pronounced "coom."

Dehydration The loss of water from the body.

Face One side of a mountain. A wall of rock or ice.

Glacier A large mass of ice that starts from a build-up of snow in a high valley and slowly moves down a mountain.

Gully A narrow split in the rock face.

Holds The climbers' word for small cracks in the rock face that they can grip with their hands or feet.

Monastery The home of a religious community, especially of monks, living away from normal society and following strict religious vows.

Paralysis An inability to move.

Pitons Pegs that can be hammered into a crack in a rock face or straight into ice. A rope can then be tied to the piton, anchoring the climber to the mountain.

Finding Out More

Climbing is a dangerous sport. You should not try it without being taught by an experienced climber. If you are interested, there are many climbing clubs that can help you to learn. Your local library can give you details. To find out more about Everest and other peaks in the Himalayas, call or write to the Embassy of the Republic of Nepal or of the Republic of China. The Embassy's information service will be able to help you.

You may also contact:

Appalachian Mountain Club
5 Joy Street
Boston, MA 02108

Adirondack Mountain Club
172 Ridge Street
Glens Falls, New York 12801

The Mountaineers
300 Third Ave., W.
Seattle, WA 98119

Potomac Appalachian Trail Club
1718 N Street, NW
Washington, DC 20036

Books to Read

There are many books about Everest. Most of these have been written for adults, but they usually contain many photographs and illustrations. Your local library should be able to help you to find these books.

Martyn Bramwell, *Mountains*. Franklin Watts, 1987

Dougal Dixon, *Mountains*. Franklin Watts, 1984

Keith Lye, *Take A Trip to Nepal*. Franklin Watts, 1988

John Snelling, *Buddhism*. Bookwright, 1986

Picture Acknowledgments

The publishers would like to thank the following for allowing their illustrations to be used in this book:

Aldus Archives 11 (bottom left and right); Chapel Studios 6 (bottom); Mountain Camera 6 (top), 7, 12 (bottom), 27, 29 (top and bottom); Royal Geographic Society 4, 5, 8, 9 (top left, right and bottom), 10, 11 (top), 14 (bottom), 15, 17 (left and right), 19, 26, 28; Topham *frontispiece*, 12 (top), 14 (top). All maps are by Peter Bull.

Index

Page numbers in *italics* refer to illustrations